NATIONAL PARK SERVICE HISTORY SERIES

CAMPAIGN FOR PETERSBURG

RICHARD WAYNE LYKES

CW2

National Park Service
U.S. Department of the Interior
Washington, D.C. 1970

For sale by the Superintendent of Documents,
U.S. Government Printing Office
Washington, D.C. 20402 - Price $1.60
S/N 024-005-00253-7
Cat. No. I 29.58/2:P44

CONTENTS

In the final year of the Civil War in the East, the fighting focused upon Petersburg, an important transportation center for Richmond and Lee's army. For 10 bloody months of combat, both from behind prepared positions and along the main routes of supply, Lee's ragged Confederates held the city (shown here from north of the Appomattox River) against Grant's numerically superior Federals. On April 2–3, 1865, Lee was forced to abandon both Petersburg and Richmond. One week later, he surrendered the Army of Northern Virginia at Appomattox Court House, dooming the South's bid for independent existence.

1

PROLOGUE

By June 1864, when the siege of Petersburg began, the Civil War had lain heavily on both the North and the South for more than 3 years. Most of the fighting in the East during this period had taken place on the rolling Virginia countryside between the opposing capitals of Washington and Richmond, only 110 miles apart, and all of it had failed to end the war and bring peace to the land. Various generals had been placed in command of the Union's mighty Army of the Potomac and had faced Gen. Robert E. Lee's Army of Northern Virginia. So far not one had succeeded in destroying Lee's army or in capturing Richmond.

Perhaps Maj. Gen. George B. McClellan had come the closest to success when, in the late spring and early summer of 1862, his Northern troops had threatened the Confederate capital, only to be repulsed on its outskirts. The other Northern commanders who followed McClellan—Pope, Burnside, Hooker, and Meade—were less successful. Lee had met and turned aside their drives.

After 36 months of bitter conflict the war in the East seemed, to many observers, to be far from a final settlement. The failure of Union forces to deliver a decisive blow against the Army of Northern Virginia was a source of growing concern in Washington. The Confederacy, for its part, was no more successful in settling the issue. Attempted invasions of the Northern States by Lee were turned back at Antietam in September 1862 and at Gettysburg in July 1863.

Farther west the picture was brighter for Northern hopes. In the same month as the Battle of Gettysburg, the Confederate stronghold of Vicksburg, Miss., fell into Union hands. A few days later, Port Hudson, La., the last remaining stronghold of the Confederacy on the banks of the Mississippi River, surrendered. Later in 1863, the Union capture of Chattanooga, Tenn., threw open the gateway to Georgia.

Strategically, despite the stalemate in Virginia, the beginning of 1864 found the Northern armies in a stronger position than the Confederate military forces. Not only was there a distinct possibility that the Southern States east of the Mississippi could be split into two parts, but the greater resources at the command of the Lincoln ad-

From the Rapidan River to the James, Lt. Gen. Ulysses S. Grant (above), commanding the armies of the United States, found all his efforts to capture Richmond and destroy the Confederacy blocked by Gen. Robert E. Lee (left) and his Army of Northern Virginia. Finally, Grant turned his attention to Petersburg.

ministration were beginning to count more heavily with each passing day. All that seemed to be needed to end the war was an able Union commander who could marshal the mighty resources of his country for a last tremendous blow at the South.

Such a man was found in Maj. Gen. Ulysses S. Grant, the victor at Vicksburg and Missionary Ridge, who was brought east and, on March 9, 1864, commissioned lieutenant general to be responsible for all the Union armies. Unlike his predecessor, Henry W. Halleck, Grant decided not to remain in Washington but chose instead to accompany the Army of the Potomac, where he would provide general direction to the military operations but leave the execution of them to that army's commander, Maj. Gen. George G. Meade.

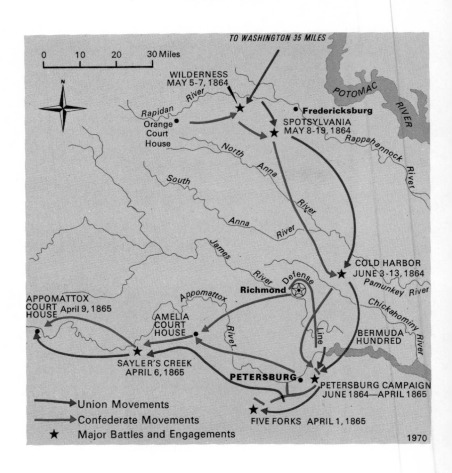

TO WASHINGTON 35 MILES

0   10   20   30 Miles

WILDERNESS
MAY 5-7, 1864

Rapidan River

Orange
Court
House

Fredericksburg

SPOTSYLVANIA
MAY 8-19, 1864

Rappahannock River

POTOMAC RIVER

North Anna River

South Anna River

COLD HARBOR
JUNE 3-13, 1864

Pamunkey River

James River

Defense Line

Richmond

Chickahominy River

APPOMATTOX
COURT HOUSE April 9, 1865

Appomattox River

AMELIA
COURT
HOUSE

BERMUDA
HUNDRED

SAYLER'S CREEK
APRIL 6, 1865

PETERSBURG

PETERSBURG CAMPAIGN
JUNE 1864—APRIL 1865

Union Movements

Confederate Movements

★   Major Battles and Engagements

FIVE FORKS   APRIL 1, 1865

1970

Maj. Gen. George G. Meade commanded the Army of the Potomac during the 1864–65 Virginia campaign. With General Grant actively directing most of the military operations, Meade was in the awkward position of serving much like a corps commander in his own army. He nevertheless functioned well in this difficult situation.

UNION STRATEGY 1864

To accomplish the conquest of the Confederacy, the Northern plan called for a huge two-pronged attack. Maj. Gen. William T. Sherman, in command of the southern prong, was assigned the task of destroying Gen. Joseph E. Johnston's Confederate Army of Tennessee, capturing Atlanta, marching to the sea, and then turning north to effect a junction with Grant.

It was the upper arm of the movement which was directly concerned with Richmond and Petersburg. This was composed of two armies: the Army of the Potomac and the Army of the James. It was the task of these armies to capture Richmond, crush the Army of Northern Virginia, and march south toward Sherman.

The story of the Army of the James in the early phase of the offensive can be briefly told. Maj. Gen. Benjamin F. Butler was ordered to advance upon Richmond from the southeast and threaten communications between the Confederate capital and the Southern States. With some 40,000 Union troops, the advance was begun. City Point, located at the junction of the James and Appomattox Rivers and soon to be the supply center for the attack on Petersburg, was captured on May 4, 1864. Within 2 weeks, however, a numerically inferior Confederate force shut up the Army of the James, "as if it had been in a bottle strongly corked," in Bermuda Hundred, a loop formed by the winding James and Appomattox Rivers. Here Butler waited, while north of him the Army of the Potomac and the Army of Northern Virginia engaged in a series of bloody battles.

The Battle of the Wilderness, May 5–7, 1864, began what proved to be the start of the final campaign against the Army of Northern Virginia. Here Meade's Army of the Potomac, numbering approximately 118,000 troops, fought the Confederate defenders of Richmond. Lee had about 62,000 men with him, while an additional 30,000 under Gen. P. G. T. Beauregard held the Richmond-Petersburg area. The battle resulted in a fearful loss of men on both sides, although the armies remained intact. This was followed by a series of fierce engagements around Spotsylvania Court House from May 8 to 21.

Failing to destroy the Army of Northern Virginia in these battles, Grant moved the Army of the Potomac to the east of Richmond. It was his hope that he would outflank the Confederate defenders by persistent night marches. Lee was not to be so easily outguessed, however. After minor battles at the North Anna River (May 23) and Totopotomoy Creek (May 29), Grant arrived at Cold Harbor, about 8 miles northeast of Richmond, but Lee's army still stood between him and that city. On June 3, 2 days after he arrived at Cold Harbor, Grant ordered a direct frontal assault against the Confederate lines. He was repulsed with heavy losses— about 7,000 men. "I have always regretted that the last assault at Cold Harbor was ever made," Grant would write many years later.

By the end of the first month of Grant's campaign, both sides had suffered heavy casualties, but the North's ability to refill its depleted ranks was greater than the South's. Lee's offensive strength had been sapped. From the Battle of Spotsylvania Court House until the end of the war, except for counterattacks and the lunge at Fort Stedman during the siege of Petersburg, the Army of Northern Virginia was a defensive weapon only.

After Cold Harbor, Grant decided to turn quickly to the south of Richmond and isolate the city and the defending troops by attacking Petersburg and cutting the railroads that supplied them. Lee knew he could not allow this to happen. "We must destroy this army of Grant's before he gets to James River," he told one of his generals. "If he gets there, it will become a siege, and then it will be a mere question of time."

STRATEGIC PETERSBURG

According to the United States census of 1860, Petersburg was a city of 18,266 people. It was situated on the southern bank of the Appomattox River about 8 miles from City Point, where the Appomattox joins the James, and 23 miles south of Richmond. As the war progressed and the territory to the north and east was shut off, Richmond became increasingly dependent on Petersburg for supplies. Through it passed a constant stream of war materials and necessities of life from the South to sustain the straining war effort. In short, Petersburg was a road and rail center of vital importance to the Confederacy, and its capture would almost certainly lead to the abandonment of Richmond.

The transportation vehicles of the 1860's did not require the wide, straight highways of the present. However, several good roads came into the city from the east, south, and west where they joined with the Richmond Turnpike. Along these roads passed supply wagons, couriers, and, on occasion, troops on their way to repel the foe. Several were built of logs laid across the road to form a hard surface. Because of this they were called "plank roads." Two of the most important arteries of traffic into Petersburg were the Jerusalem Plank Road, connecting Petersburg with Jerusalem (now Courtland),

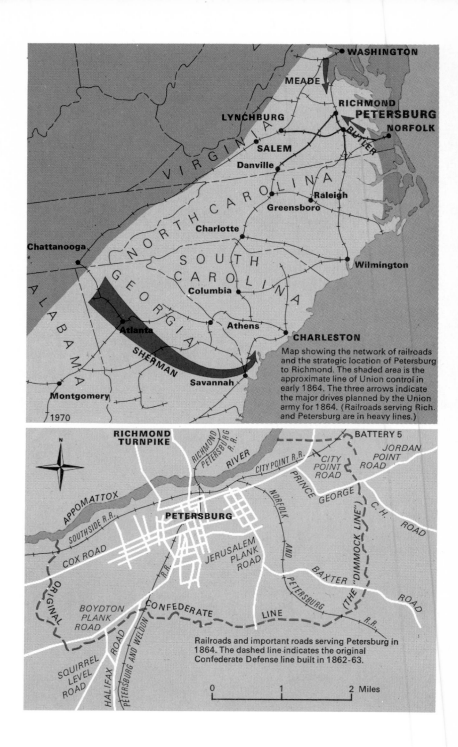

Map showing the network of railroads and the strategic location of Petersburg to Richmond. The shaded area is the approximate line of Union control in early 1864. The three arrows indicate the major drives planned by the Union army for 1864. (Railroads serving Rich. and Petersburg are in heavy lines.)

Railroads and important roads serving Petersburg in 1864. The dashed line indicates the original Confederate Defense line built in 1862-63.

0   1   2 Miles

Va., and the Boydton Plank Road which led south through Dinwiddie Court House. Among others of importance were the City Point, Prince George Court House, Baxter, Halifax, Jordon Point, Squirrel Level, and Cox Roads.

It was the railroads more than the highways, however, which gave to Petersburg a significance out of all proportion to its size. Tracks radiated from the city in all directions. The Richmond and Petersburg Railroad left the city to the north; the Southside Railroad ran west to Lynchburg; the Petersburg and Weldon Railroad led south to North Carolina; the Norfolk and Petersburg Railroad passed through a ravine east of the city before turning southeast toward Norfolk; and the Petersburg and City Point Railroad struck out for the hamlet of City Point, situated at the junction of the James and Appomattox Rivers about 8 miles away.

Because of its proximity, Petersburg became a part of the transportation system of the Confederate capital, serving as a major point of transfer to the larger metropolis for products and materials from the vast regions to the south and southwest. By June 1864, all but one railroad from the south and west into Richmond—the Richmond and Danville Railroad—passed through Petersburg. As other lines of supply were cut off or threatened, the dependence of Richmond upon Petersburg increased and made the security of that city a matter of vital concern.

In the spring of 1862, McClellan's Peninsular Campaign had threatened Richmond from the east and southeast, making that city's defenders acutely aware of the need for a system of fortifications around Petersburg. In August a defense line was begun, and work continued until its completion about a year later. Capt. Charles H. Dimmock, a Northerner by birth, was in charge of it under the direction of the Engineer Bureau, Confederate States Army, and the line so constructed became unofficially known as the "Dimmock Line."

When finished, the chain of breastworks and artillery emplacements around Petersburg was 10 miles long, beginning and ending on the Appomattox River and protecting all but the northern approaches to the city. The

55 artillery batteries were consecutively numbered from east to west. Although natural terrain features were utilized whenever possible, some glaring weaknesses existed, such as the deep ravine between Batteries 7 and 8, which could provide a means of penetration by an attacking force. The very length and size of the fortifications proved to be a disadvantage. It meant that a larger number of troops would be necessary to defend the line than General Beauregard, charged with this heavy responsibility, had present for duty. Col. Alfred Roman, an aide-de-camp to Beauregard, estimated that the long "Dimmock Line" would require more than 10 times as many men to defend it as were available.

On several occasions raids were made on the railroads south and west of Petersburg. The most serious of these occurred on June 9, 1864, when 3,000 infantry and 1,300 cavalry appeared in force along the eastern and southeastern sector of the Dimmock Line. The infantry contented itself with a menacing demonstration, but the cavalry attacked up the Jerusalem Plank Road. After breaking through the defenses, the horse soldiers were checked by regular Southern army units assisted by a hastily summoned home guard of old men and youths. The damage done by such raids was quickly patched up, but they were a constant nuisance to the city's transportation lines. To shut off permanently the supplies that streamed along the railroads, the Union forces would have to take permanent physical possession of them.

BATTLE OF PETERSBURG

After the Battle of Cold Harbor on June 3, Grant had abandoned, for a time at least, his plan to capture Richmond by direct assault. With characteristic zeal he had ordered Meade to move the Army of the Potomac across the James River and to invest the more southerly city. On June 14, Grant and Butler conferred at Bermuda Hundred. At that time, orders were given for the attack on Petersburg.

The first of the Northern forces to arrive on the scene of battle was the XVIII Corps of the Army of the James, which had fought at Cold Harbor. Early in the morning of June 15, these troops, commanded by Maj. Gen. W.

F. "Baldy" Smith, crossed from Bermuda Hundred to the south side of the Appomattox by means of a pontoon bridge at Broadway Landing. Eighteen thousand Union soldiers were on their way to face less than 4,000 under Beauregard. Throughout the day they approached the city and assembled for the attack.

There was skirmishing throughout the afternoon as the Federals drove in the Confederate pickets, and shortly after 7 p.m. on June 15 the XVIII Corps launched a fierce attack on the Dimmock Line. Among the first points to fall was Battery 5, one of the strongest of the Confederate positions. Within a few hours Beauregard

Gen. P. G. T. Beauregard, Confederate commander at Petersburg during the early days of the campaign, defended the "Dimmock Line" against the Federal assaults of June 15–18, 1864. When Lee arrived to direct operations, Beauregard's troops were merged with the Army of Northern Virginia.

had lost not only Battery 5 but all the line for more than a mile south. The defenders withdrew and threw up a hasty entrenchment behind Harrison's Creek, well to the rear of the captured section of the line. While the Confederate retreat was taking place, the Union II Corps, commanded by Maj. Gen. Winfield S. Hancock, arrived to reinforce the Federal columns.

The appearance on the field of the II Corps was an ominous sign for the Confederates. While the initial attacks were taking place on June 15, the Army of the Potomac had been busily engaged in crossing the James River farther to the east. The number of Union troops south of the river was increasing hourly, until by midnight of June 16 at least 70,000 had crossed.

Darkness ended the fighting on June 15, but early the next day the attacks were renewed. More of the defense line south of the portion captured the previous day, now gave way. In response to repeated entreaties from Beauregard throughout June 15 and 16, Lee ordered more divisions to the support of Petersburg, necessitating the draining of precious reserves from the Richmond lines. By dawn of that second day, Beauregard could muster about 14,000 men to face the enemy. Thus, the center of attention rapidly shifted from Richmond to Petersburg, which had so recently seemed of but secondary importance.

1. *Broadway Landing on the Appomattox River where Maj. Gen. W. F. "Baldy" Smith's XVIII Corps of the Army of the James crossed on June 15, 1864. It was later used as an ordnance depot by the Union Army.*

2. *Pontoon bridge at Broadway Landing constructed by Federal soldiers in 1864.*

3. *Confederate Battery 5, shown here under Federal occupation 6 days after its capture, was one of the first points on Petersburg's outer defense lines to fall to the XVIII Corps during the June 15 attack.*

2

3

The third day of battle was practically a repetition of that of the preceding day. Again the Northern forces attacked the Confederate troops, concentrating their efforts to the south of the positions captured earlier. Again the Confederates were forced to draw back. A decisive breakthrough of the opposing line was now anticipated by the assaulting forces. About 12:30 a.m., June 18, Beauregard ordered his troops to begin a withdrawal to new positions about a mile closer to the city. Throughout the early morning hours of that day Beauregard had his men busily engaged in the construction of this defense line. Colonel Roman later recalled that "without a moment's rest the digging of the trenches was begun, with such utensils as had been hastily collected

A section of the Confederate defense lines around Petersburg. Note the use of wickerware (gabions), sharpened stakes (fraises), and branches (abatis) to protect the position.

at Petersburg, many of the men using their bayonets, their knives, and even their tin cans, to assist in the rapid execution of the work."

A general assault by the Union forces was ordered for 4 a.m. on June 18. When the attack began it was soon discovered that the ranks of the enemy had not been broken nor had the city fallen into Northern hands. The area where the left flank of the Dimmock Line anchored on the Appomattox was empty, except for a thin line of skirmishers who were gradually forced back. The Northern troops came on, crossing the Norfolk and Petersburg Railroad west of where the defenders had constructed their new line and continuing on until they were

15

brought face to face with the muzzles of Confederate guns. Meanwhile, elements of Lee's command continued pouring in to aid their comrades, and Lee came down from his temporary headquarters near Chester, Va., to personally direct the defense operations.

Throughout that June Saturday, brisk action occurred on the new Petersburg front. The major Union drive, involving elements of five corps, came about 4 p.m. Artillery hammered the Confederates. Infantry charged, only to be hurled back. During the course of one of these futile drives, the 1st Maine Heavy Artillery reportedly suffered the most severe losses of any regiment in a single engagement of the entire war. This unit, 850 strong, charged from the concealment of the Prince George Court House Road north of where Fort Stedman was soon to stand. Met by a heavy crossfire, it withdrew in less than one-half hour, with 632 casualties.

As on the previous days, fighting ended with the coming of darkness. Grant's attempt to capture Petersburg had failed, with a loss of 10,000 men; but his efforts could not be considered entirely wasted. Two of the railroads leading into the city had been cut, and several roads were in Union hands. Behind the Northern troops was City Point, which Grant speedily converted into a huge supply base.

The major result of the opening 4 days of combat, however, was the failure of the Federal forces to break the Confederate defense line. First Beauregard, and then Lee, had held against heavy odds. They had been pushed back closer to their base—but they had held. Possibly if Smith had advanced his XVIII Corps farther into the defenses on the opening night, or if Hancock's II Corps had arrived earlier, Petersburg would have fallen on June 15 or 16. But these had not happened, and now 47,000 to 51,000 Confederates would settle down to defend the city against 111,000 to 113,000 Union besiegers.

The defenses of Richmond now ran from White Oak Swamp, east of that city, south to Jerusalem Plank Road, 26 miles away. The fate of the Army of Northern Virginia—of the Confederate capital itself—would depend upon the outcome of the drive against Petersburg.

The Union Army, having failed in its initial attack on Petersburg, was now committed to doing something further to effect its capture. From June 19 to July 9, the Union forces were engaged in three kinds of activity. First, elements of the army were set to work consolidating the positions captured in the 4-day battle and constructing the devices needed for siege operations. Second, jabbing cavalry thrusts were made at the important supply routes into Petersburg. And third, they reconnoitered the Confederate defenses to determine a plan which would force Lee out of his lines.

A threatening movement toward the Weldon Railroad was promptly undertaken by the Northern troops. Three days after the failure to capture the city, two corps (the II and VI) began to push to the southwest of Grant's flank on the Jerusalem Plank Road. The following day, June 22, Confederate divisions led by Generals Cadmus M. Wilcox and William Mahone advanced from the defense line south of Petersburg and rolled by the Federals, capturing 1,700 prisoners, four cannons, and eight stands of colors.

FIRST UNION ATTEMPT TO ENCIRCLE PETERSBURG

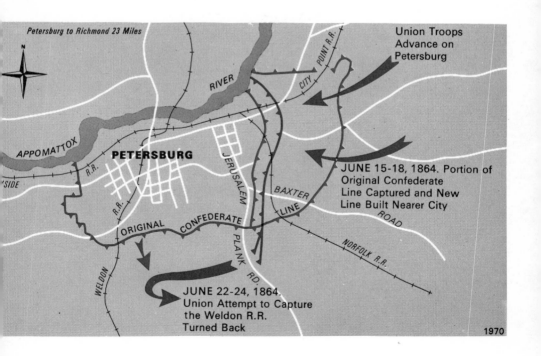

Petersburg to Richmond 23 Miles

N

RIVER

CITY POINT R.R.

Union Troops Advance on Petersburg

APPOMATTOX

'SIDE

R.R.

PETERSBURG

JERUSALEM

BAXTER LINE

JUNE 15-18, 1864. Portion of Original Confederate Line Captured and New Line Built Nearer City

ROAD

R.R.

ORIGINAL CONFEDERATE

PLANK RD.

WELDON

NORFOLK R.R.

JUNE 22-24, 1864. Union Attempt to Capture the Weldon R.R. Turned Back

1970

The next morning saw the resumption of the advance toward the Weldon Railroad. A Union patrol succeeded in reaching the tracks on the 23d and promptly started the work of destruction. Alarmed by the threat to this important supply line, the Confederates launched a sharp attack that forced the withdrawal of the Union forces from the vicinity of the railroad. However, the Union lines confronting Petersburg had been extended across the Jerusalem Plank Road, thus cutting off its use to the city.

In itself, the Battle of Jerusalem Plank Road on June 22–24 was not too important militarily. The North could quickly replace the loss of 2,300 men. The Weldon Railroad, although its days were numbered, was still able to deliver supplies to Petersburg. But as an indication of Grant's tactics, it pointed the course of the campaign ahead. It marked the first of several attempts to encircle

Destruction of Genl. Lee's lines of comm

Petersburg, and the others to follow would not all be as disappointing to Northern hopes. In these repeated drives to the west lay the essence of the basic plan to capture Petersburg.

On July 9, the plan of operations decided upon by the Union high command was revealed in an order from Meade's headquarters giving detailed instructions for the building of fortifications and the development of siege tactics. It thus became apparent that the Union plan was to reduce Petersburg by a process of attrition —a process that was to last for 9 months.

There were still those in the attacking forces, however, who felt that, with a little imagination, the city could be taken by direct assault. While most of the troops were digging siege lines, another smaller group had already begun work on a unique plan which would, if successful, make further encirclement unnecessary.

The Federal cavalry saw little battle action during the siege, but it did its share in destroying Lee's lines of communication. Combat artist Alfred R. Waud of Harper's Weekly *made this sketch of Brig. Gen. James H. Wilson's troopers tearing up part of the Weldon Railroad, south of Petersburg, during their June 1864 raid.*

The "Dictator," also called
"The Petersburg Express,"
was a 17,000-pound, 13-inch
Federal seacoast mortar
mounted on a reinforced
railroad car. During the early
part of the siege, this huge
weapon fired 200-pound
explosive shells into
Petersburg, 2½ miles away,
from a curved section of the
Petersburg and City Point
Railroad. On July 30, 1864, it
was part of the artillery support
for Union troops during
the Battle of the Crater.

1

2

3

1. The men who commanded the "Dictator"—Col. H. L. Abbot (the man on the left in front) and officers of the 1st Connecticut Heavy Artillery. Next to Abbot is Maj. Gen. Henry J. Hunt, in charge of all artillery operations on the Petersburg front.

2. The "Dictator" in permanent position near Union Battery IV, formerly Confederate Battery 5.

3. A 13-inch seacoast mortar on display at Petersburg National Battlefield today, on the site where the "Dictator" stood during most of the siege.

BATTLE OF THE CRATER

At several places east of the city the opposing lines were extremely close together. One of these locations was in front of Pegram's (sometimes called Elliott's) Salient, a Confederate strong point near old Blandford Church. Here the Confederate position on Cemetery Hill and the Union picket line were less than 400 feet apart. Because of the proximity of the Union line, Pegram's Salient was well fortified. Behind earthen embankments was a battery of four guns, and two veteran South Carolina infantry regiments were stationed on either side. Behind these were other defensive works; before them the ground sloped gently downward toward the Union advance line.

This forward Union line was built on the crest of a ravine which had been crossed on June 18. Through this ravine, and between the sentry line and the main line, lay the roadbed of the Norfolk and Petersburg Railroad. The front in this sector was manned by Maj. Gen. Ambrose E. Burnside's IX Corps. Among the many units which composed this corps was the 48th Regiment, Pennsylvania Veteran Volunteer Infantry. A large proportion of this regiment was made up of onetime coal miners, and it apparently occurred to one or more of them that Pegram's Salient would provide an excellent place to use their civilian knowhow. Lt. Col. Henry Pleasants, the commanding officer of the 48th and a mining engineer by profession, overheard one of the enlisted men mutter, "We could blow that damned fort out of existence if we could run a mine shaft under it." From this and similar remarks came the germ of the idea for a Union mine.

The 48th Regiment proposed to dig a long gallery from the bottom of the ravine behind their picket line to a point beneath the Confederate battery at Pegram's Salient, blow up the position by powder placed in the end of the tunnel, and then send a strong body of troops through the gap created in the enemy's line by the explosion. They saw as the reward for their effort the capitulation of Petersburg and, perhaps, the end of the war.

After obtaining the permission of Burnside and Grant, Pleasants and his men commenced digging their mine shaft on June 25. The lack of proper equipment made it necessary to improvise tools and apparatus with which

*Lt. Col. Henry Pleasants,
onetime mining engineer and
the commanding officer of the
48th Pennsylvania Regiment
which dug the tunnel
under the Confederate line.*

to excavate. Mining picks were created by straightening army picks. Cracker boxes were converted into hand-barrows in which the dirt was removed from the end of the tunnel. A sawmill changed a bridge into timber necessary for shoring up the mine. Pleasants estimated the tunnel's direction and depth by means of a theodolite sent him from Washington. The instrument, although outmoded, served its purpose well: the mine shaft hit exactly beneath the salient at which it was aimed.

One of the most remarkable features of the gallery was the method devised to supply the diggers at the end with fresh air. The longer the tunnel grew, the more serious the problem of ventilation became. It had been considered impossible to dig a tunnel for any considerable distance without spacing shafts at regular intervals in

CONFEDERATE LINE

JULY 30, 1864,
Pegram's Battery destroyed
by explosion

JULY 27, 1864,
8,000 lbs. of powder
placed here

Air tube

510-8/10 feet

Cross-section view of the Federal tunnel under the Confederate line. Colonel Pleasants later recalled that "General Burnside told me that General Meade and Major Duane, chief engineer of the Army of the Potomac, said the thing could not be done—that it was all clap-trap and nonsense; that such a length of mine had never been excavated in military operations, and could not be; that I would either get the men smothered, for want of air, or crushed by the falling of the earth; or the enemy would find it out and it would amount to nothing."

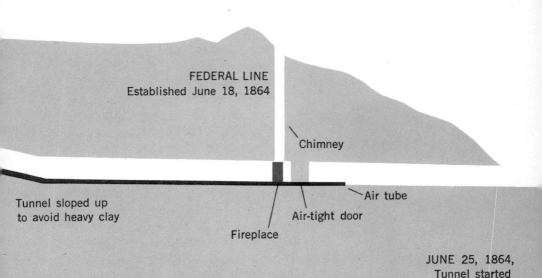

FEDERAL LINE
Established June 18, 1864

Chimney

Air tube

Tunnel sloped up
to avoid heavy clay

Air-tight door

Fireplace

JUNE 25, 1864,
Tunnel started

order to replace the polluted air with a fresh supply. This problem had been solved by the application of the simple physical principle that warm air rises. Behind the Union picket line and to the right of the mine gallery, although connected with it, the miners dug a ventilating chimney. Between the chimney and the mine entrance they erected an airtight canvas door. Through that door and along the floor of the gallery they laid a square wooden pipe. A fire was then built at the bottom of the ventilating shaft. As the fire warmed the air it went up the chimney. The draft thus created drew the bad air from the end of the tunnel where the men were digging. As this went out, fresh air was drawn in through the wooden pipe to replace it.

Work on the tunnel continued steadily from June 25, and by July 17 the diggers were nearly 511 feet from the entrance and directly beneath the battery in Pegram's Salient. The Confederates had learned of the mine by this time and had dug several countermines behind their own lines in an effort to locate the Union gallery. Two were very close, being dug on either side of where the Pennsylvanians were at work. Although digging in the countermines continued throughout July, Confederate fears seemed to lessen during the same period. There were many reasons for this, one being the failure of their tunnels to strike any Union construction. Another major reason, undoubtedly, was a belief held by many that it was impossible to ventilate a shaft of any length over 400 feet without constructing air shafts along it, and so far no air shafts could be seen between the Union and Confederate lines.

The next step in the Union plan was to burrow out into lateral galleries at the end of the long shaft. Accordingly, on July 18, work was begun on these branches which extended to the right and left, paralleling the Confederate fortifications above. When completed, these added another 75 feet to the total length of the tunnel which now reached 586 feet into the earth. It was about 20 feet from the floor of the tunnel to the enemy works above. The average internal dimensions of the shaft were 5 feet high, with a base 4½ feet wide tapering to 2 feet at the top.

Digging was finally completed on July 23. Four days later the task of charging the mine with black powder was accomplished. Three hundred and twenty kegs of powder weighing about 25 pounds each were arranged in the two lateral galleries in eight magazines. The total charge was 8,000 pounds. The powder was sandbagged to direct the force of the explosion upward and the fuses were spliced together to form a 98-foot line.

Meanwhile, preparations for the large-scale attack which was to follow the explosion of the mine had been carried out. Burnside wanted his IX Corps to lead the attack, spearheaded by a fresh, 4,300-man Negro division, and pressed his wishes on Meade. Both Meade and Grant approved the request, but refused to allow the black troops to lead the assault for fear that, if the attack failed, the Union commanders could be accused of wanting to get rid of the only Negro troops then with the Army of the Potomac. Burnside did not learn of this decision until the day before the assault, July 29, and he was forced to change his plans at the last moment. Three white divisions would make the initial charge, with the black division in reserve. Burnside had the commanding generals of these three divisions draw straws to see which would lead. Brig. Gen. James F. Ledlie of the 1st Division won the draw.

Despite these 11th-hour changes, a plan of battle had been evolved. During the night of July 29–30, the bulk of the IX Corps was assembled in the ravine behind the mine entrance and in the two approach trenches leading to the picket line. Troops from other Union corps were marshalled as reinforcements. Artillerymen, manning 110 guns and 54 mortars, were alerted to begin shelling the Confederate line. To assist the attack, Grant sent a cavalry and infantry force north of the James to threaten the Richmond defenses and destroy whatever they could of the Virginia Central Railroad. The object was to draw as many of Lee's soldiers away from Petersburg as possible. And it worked. When the assault came, only 18,000 Confederates were left to guard the city.

At 3:15 a.m., July 30, Pleasants lit the powder fuse and mounted the parapet to see the results of his regiment's work. The explosion was expected at 3:30 a.m. Time passed slowly and the men, huddled behind the lines, grew more apprehensive. By 4:15 there could be no doubt that something had gone wrong. Two volunteers from the 48th Regiment (Lt. Jacob Douty and Sgt. Harry Reese) crawled into the tunnel and found that the fuse had burned out at a splice. They relighted it and scrambled to safety. Finally, at 4:40 a.m., the earth trembled, and with one great roar, men, equipment, and debris were hurled high into the air. At least 278 Confederate troops were killed or wounded in the tremendous blast, and two of the four guns in the battery were destroyed beyond repair. The crater torn by the powder was at least 170 feet long, 60 to 80 feet wide, and 30 feet deep.

The awesome spectacle of the mine explosion caused a delay in the Union charge following the explosion. Removal of obstructions between the lines caused further delay. Soon, however, an advance was made to the crater, where many of the attacking force paused to seek shelter on its steep slopes or to look at the havoc caused by the mine. The hard-pressed Confederates rallied quickly and soon were pouring shells and minié balls into their opponents. Union reinforcements poured into the breach; but, instead of going forward, they either joined their comrades in the crater or branched out to the immediate right and left along the lines. By 8:30 that morning a large part of the IX Corps had been poured into the captured enemy salient. More than 15,000 troops now milled in and about the crater.

By prompt action and determined effort the Confederates had prevented a breakthrough. The attention of three batteries was soon directed on the bluecoats at the crater. Artillery hammered with shot and shell the huddled groups of increasingly demoralized men. In addition, mortars brought to within 50 yards of the crater dropped shells on the soldiers with deadly effect.

Successful as these devices were in halting the Union advance, Lee was aware that an infantry charge would be necessary to dislodge the enemy. By 6 a.m. an order had gone out to Brig Gen. William Mahone to move two brigades of his division from the lines south of Peters-

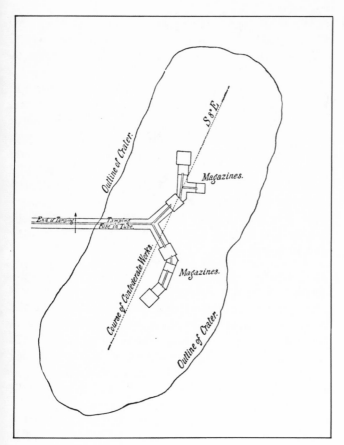

Colonel Pleasants' sketch of the Crater.

burg to the defense of the threatened position; Mahone had anticipated the order and already had his troops in motion. Then Lee joined Beauregard in observing the battle from the Gee house, 500 yards to the rear of the scene of action.

In spite of the Confederate resistance, part of the Northern black division and other regiments had, by 8 a.m., advanced a short distance beyond their companions at the crater. Shortly thereafter, Mahone's lead Confederate brigade arrived on the scene. The men filed into a ravine about 200 yards northwest of the crater and between it and Petersburg. No sooner had they entered this protected position than, perceiving the danger to their lines, they charged across the open field into the mass of Federal soldiers. Although outnumbered, they

forced the Northerners to flee back to the comparative shelter of the crater. Then they swept on to regain a portion of the line north of the Union-held position.

By 10:30 another of Mahone's brigades had reached the point of danger, and it charged the Union troops holding the crater, only to be repulsed. Meanwhile, the lot of the Northern soldiers was rapidly becoming unbearable. Confederate artillery continued to beat upon them. The closely packed troops (dead, dying, and living indiscriminately mixed) lacked shade from the blazing sun, food, water and, above all, competent leadership. Meade had ordered their withdrawal more than an hour before the second Confederate charge, but Burnside delayed the transmission of the order till after midday. Many men had chosen to run the gantlet of fire back to their own lines, but others remained clinging to the protective sides of the crater.

The last scene in the battle occurred shortly after 1 p.m.

Mahone had called up a third brigade, and an attack spearheaded by the fresh unit succeeded in gaining the slopes of the crater. Some of the Union men, overcome with exhaustion and realizing the helplessness of their situation, surrendered; but others continued to fight. At one point where resistance centered, the Confederates put their hats on ramrods and lifted them over the rim of the crater. The caps were promptly torn to shreds by a volley of minié balls. Before their foe could reload, Mahone's forces jumped into the crater where a desperate struggle with bayonets, rifle butts, and fists ensued.

Soon it was all over. The Union army had lost more than 4,000 men killed, wounded, or captured, as against about 1,500 for the Confederates. Again, as on June 15–18, a frontal assault had failed to take the Confederate stronghold, even though Union numerical strength greatly exceeded that of the Confederates. At the battle's close Grant had more than 83,000 men south of the Appomattox River; Lee had about 22,000.

What 8,000 pounds of powder could do—the crater as it appeared in 1865. The Union soldier seated at the end of the tunnel gives an idea of the crater's size.

FIGHT FOR THE WELDON RAILROAD

Grant, if he reviewed the fruits of his campaign shortly after July 30, could not have felt much comfort. Three hammering blows delivered against Petersburg had failed. Moreover, two important railroads still connected the city with the South. Lee, despite his numerically inferior numbers, was still able to maintain a long line of defenses around Petersburg and Richmond. Farther south, the Union outlook was brighter. Ten days before the Battle of the Crater, final operations against Atlanta had been begun by Sherman. On September 2 it was to fall, and the march to the sea followed in 10 weeks.

Yet it was equally certain that Grant had accomplished an important objective. By committing Lee's weakened but still potent Army of Northern Virginia to a defensive position in the area adjacent to Richmond, he was immobilizing the South's most powerful striking force. Moreover, the Union failure at the crater decided the future direction of the campaign to capture Petersburg. All Grant's energy now turned to extending his siege lines around the city and cutting Lee's supply lines in an attempt to force him out of his defenses.

The first step taken in this direction after July 30 was a strong effort to capture the Weldon Railroad, which the Confederates had so nearly lost in June. On August 16, Maj. Gen. Gouverneur K. Warren, Union V Corps commander, received orders to attack, occupy, and hold the Weldon Railroad 3 miles below the city.

The seizure of the objective was quickly accomplished on August 18, the opening day of battle. More than a mile of track near Globe Tavern, an old colonial inn, was soon in Union hands. Then Warren marched most of his troops northward toward the city. They were in unfamiliar and heavily wooded terrain where they were assailed by two Confederate brigades led by Maj. Gen. Henry Heth. The Union troops were forced to fall back a short distance and entrench. Here the V Corps was reinforced by the IX Corps.

On the afternoon of the 19th, five brigades of Lt. Gen. A. P. Hill's Corps struck the Union infantry. Three of the brigades under Mahone managed to slip in behind their opponents by taking advantage of the concealment offered. by the heavy growth of trees. They inflicted

Globe Tavern, near the Weldon Railroad. During the Battle for the Weldon Railroad, August 18–21, 1864, this building was headquarters for Maj. Gen. Gouverneur K. Warren's V Corps.

serious losses and captured 2,500 prisoners. By nightfall, Warren had been forced back one-half mile nearer his new headquarters at Globe Tavern.

August 20 was marked by comparative inactivity, although there was some skirmishing in the morning. Throughout the following day A. P. Hill, who had received reinforcements, threw his men at the Union positons around the tavern. The attacks were in vain, for the new Union lines held. General Lee arrived with more infantry brigades during the afternoon, but after discussing the situation with his generals, he determined not to renew the attack. By the end of the day Lee realized that the upper portion of the Weldon Railroad had been lost and that any attempt to regain it would be a needless sacrifice of manpower.

Cattle Raid
+ R. Wand

One sentence from a dispatch sent by Lee to the Confederate Secretary of War on August 22 shows the seriousness of the loss of the railroad: "Our supply of corn is exhausted today, and I am informed that the small reserve in Richmond is consumed." For a time the Confederate government was able to utilize the Weldon Railroad as far as Stony Creek, 20 miles below Petersburg, where supplies were transferred to wagons and hauled around the left of the Northern army to Petersburg and Richmond. In December the railroad line was destroyed below Stony Creek and henceforth the beleaguered cities had only two direct rail communications with the South—the Richmond and Danville Railroad out of Richmond and the Southside from Petersburg.

On August 25, 2 days after the fighting at Globe Tavern had ended, the Confederates scored a minor victory with a surprise attack. Their blow was aimed at Hancock's II Corps busily engaged in destroying railroad tracks at Reams Station, nearly 5 miles below Globe

Tavern. The II Corps, containing large numbers of inexperienced recruits, was badly beaten and more than 1,700 were taken prisoner. The Southern victory was shortlived, for the destruction of their rail communications was continued. The best that Lee could hope for in the future would be to stem the Federal advance.

In mid-September, Maj. Gen. Wade Hampton, cavalry commander of the Army of Northern Virginia since J. E. B. Stuart's death in May, led a remarkable raid of 4,000 mounted troops around the rear of the Union army, now numbering 80,000. He succeeded in returning to Petersburg on September 17 with about 2,400 head of cattle and more than 300 prisoners, while suffering losses of only 61 men in two engagements with the enemy. Although this raised the morale of the Confederates, it did not change the course of the campaign. The iron band being forged outside their city was a reality, and Grant, a tenacious man, had not loosened his grip.

Petersburg's hungry defenders were delighted when Maj. Gen. Wade Hampton's Confederate horsemen rustled more than 2,000 cattle from the Union army in September 1864. Alfred Waud sketched the raid for Harper's Weekly.

1

1. Federal soldiers in the trenches before Petersburg. By 1864, most of the men of the Armies of the Potomac and the James were veteran combat soldiers, but the strain of siege warfare eventually affected even the most hardened of them. "It was hell itself," one soldier recalled, "and it is wondrous to me that so many of us survived the event."

2. Constructing gabions for the attack on Petersburg. When filled with earth, these cylindrical, basket-like objects offered strong protection against enemy fire.

3. Federal pickets in front of Union Fort Sedgwick, opposite Confederate Fort Mahone. Note how the gabions are being used.

4. Rifled siege guns in Union Battery IV. Fire from this battery helped to seal off the Confederate breakthrough at Fort Stedman in March 1865.

5. Capt. James H. Cooper's Battery, 1st Pennsylvania Light Artillery, V Corps. While the men were standing to their guns to have this picture taken, a Confederate battery, thinking the Federals were preparing to fire, opened up on them. The famous Civil War photographer Mathew B. Brady is standing with hands in pocket beside the trail of the second gun.

UNION ENCIRCLE-MENT CONTINUES

The relentless westerly advance of the besieging force was soon resumed after the capture of the Weldon Railroad in August. Constant skirmishing occurred between the lines until, in late September, Grant struck again.

The Battle of Peebles' Farm, September 29 to October 1, was really the second section of a two-part struggle. The first took place closer to Richmond and was directed at Fort Harrison, a strongly fortified point on the outer defense line of the Confederate capital. Fort Harrison was approximately midway between Richmond and Petersburg. On the morning of September 29, Union troops advanced and captured the fort and held it the next day against a counterattack by the former occupants. At the same time, Meade was moving toward a further encirclement of Petersburg with more than 20,000 troops. The direction of his attack was northwest toward Confederate earthworks along the Squirrel Level Road. The ultimate goal was the capture of the Southside Railroad.

Fighting began on the 29th as the Federal vanguard approached the Confederates in the vicinity of Peebles' farm. The engagement increased in fury on the 30th and continued into the next day. When the smoke of battle had blown away on October 2, Meade had extended the Union left flank 3 miles farther west and had secured the ground on which Fort Fisher would soon be built. (This fort was to be the Union's biggest and was one of the largest earthern forts in Civil War history.) He was, however, stopped short of the coveted Southside Railroad. Against the gain in territory the Union army had suffered a loss of more than 1,300 prisoners to the Confederacy and more than 650 killed and wounded. The Southerners found that their lines, while unbroken, were again extended. Each extension meant a thinner Confederate defense line.

For a period of about 3 weeks after the Battle of Peebles' Farm, the shovel and pick again replaced the rifle-musket as the principal tools for soldiers on both sides. Forts were built, breastworks dug, and gabions constructed. Then, on October 27, the Union troops moved again. This time they turned toward the Boydton Plank Road and a stream known as Hatcher's Run, 12

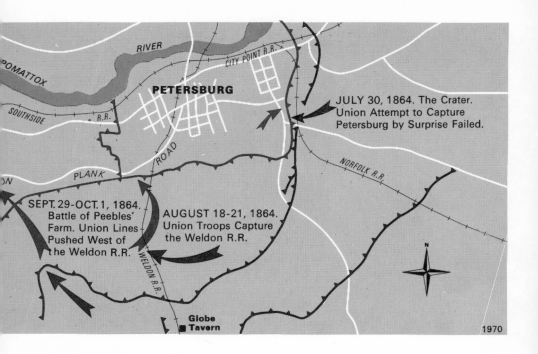

miles southwest of Petersburg. Again Grant's objective was Lee's vital supply line—the Southside Railroad.

The general plan of operations was nearly the same as that used at Peebles' farm. Butler's Army of the James was ordered to threaten attack in front of Richmond. Meanwhile, at the left of the Union line, nearly 43,000 infantry and cavalry of the Army of the Potomac started for the Boydton Plank Road. The columns made rapid progress, driving the enemy outposts ahead of them and advancing until they neared Burgess' Mill where the Boydton Plank Road crossed Hatcher's Run.

Near Burgess' Mill, heavy Confederate opposition was met and a spirited engagement took place. The failure of Union Generals Hancock of the II Corps and Warren of the V Corps to coordinate the efforts of their respective columns, coupled with a slashing thrust by Heth's infantry and dogged resistance by Hampton's cavalry and horse-artillery, resulted in a speedy Northern withdrawal. The Boydton Plank Road, for a time at least, remained in Southern hands, and Grant's encircling movement to cut Lee's railroad was checked.

The approach of winter made any large-scale effort by either side less probable, although daily skirmishes and tightening of the siege lines continued. The slackening of hostile action was used to good advantage by Union and Confederate alike, as it had been in the previous respites between battles, in the strengthening of the battlelines and efforts to develop some rudimentary comforts in the cheerless camps. Throughout the last 2 months of 1864 and the 1st month of the new year there were no strong efforts by either side before Petersburg; picket duty, sniping, and patrolling prevailed. The only action out of the trenches was the Hicksford Raid in December when a strong Union force destroyed the Weldon Railroad as far as Hicksford, about 40 miles south of Petersburg. Lee now had a 35-mile front, with the left resting on the Williamsburg Road east of Richmond and the right on Hatcher's Run southwest of Petersburg. To hold this long line he had in December an effective troop strength of only 66,533. Facing these undernourished and ragged soldiers were, according to official Union returns of the same month, 110,364 well-fed and equipped Federals.

The picture throughout the rest of the South was no more reassuring to Confederate sympathizers. In the Shenandoah Valley, northwest of Richmond, Maj. Gen. Philip H. Sheridan's army had finally crushed Lt. Gen. Jubal A. Early's Southern forces at Cedar Creek on October 19 and was destroying the scattered resistance that remained. Far to the southwest, Sherman had captured Atlanta, Ga., in September, and Savannah had surrendered on December 21. As the new year dawned, his army was prepared to march north toward Grant. To complete the gloomy Southern prospects, Fort Fisher, guardian bastion of Wilmington, N.C., the last of the Confederacy's Atlantic coast ports to remain open, was under fatal bombardment by mid-January.

In late January, President Jefferson Davis, hoping that peace might be made with the Union, agreed to send commissioners to meet with President Lincoln. The

Not everyone was shooting
all the time. Often only
handpicked sharpshooters
traded shots from the
trenches and tried to pick off
each other's artillerymen.
An artist caught these men
of the Federal XVIII Corps
at their daily, deadly business.

Peace Commissioners, on January 31, 1865, crossed over to the Union lines at Petersburg. Soldiers of both armies, suspecting their mission, cheered as the commissioners slowly walked over the scarred earth of the crater battlefield. At Hampton Roads they met Lincoln, but the "Peace Conference" ended in failure; Davis' insistence on Southern independence as a condition for peace brought about the impasse. The war continued.

The Battle of Hatcher's Run on February 5–7, 1865, was the result of a further drive by the Federals in their attempt to encircle Petersburg. Two Union corps (the II and V), reinforced by a cavalry division and elements of the VI Corps, advanced across Hatcher's Run. Their immediate objective was the Boydton Plank Road.

As had happened before, the Confederates quickly moved out to engage the Union columns. On the afternoon of the 5th, and again the next day, the Southerners counterattacked. While many Confederate units displayed their customary élan, others did not. There were several reasons for this: the inferior numbers of the Southern army, the extremely bad weather which made a Union attack appear unlikely, the ravages of cold on badly equipped and poorly uniformed men, and, most important, the breakdown of the food supply system.

The only Federal units to reach the Boydton Plank Road belonged to the cavalry, but in view of the Confederate response and the discovery that General Lee was not utilizing this road to supply his army, they were recalled. Consequently, no effort was made to hold the Boydton Plank Road, but the Federals did occupy and fortify the newly extended line to Hatcher's Run at a point 3 miles below Burgess' Mill. Thus, again the Union lines had been pushed to the west, and, as before, Lee was forced to lengthen his defenses. The Petersburg-Richmond front, with its recent extension, now stretched over 37 miles, and the army holding it had dwindled through casualties and desertion to slightly more than 56,000 on March 1, 1865.

The Battle of Hatcher's Run was another fight in the constant movement of the Union Army to the west after June 18, 1864. In its relentless extension around Peters-

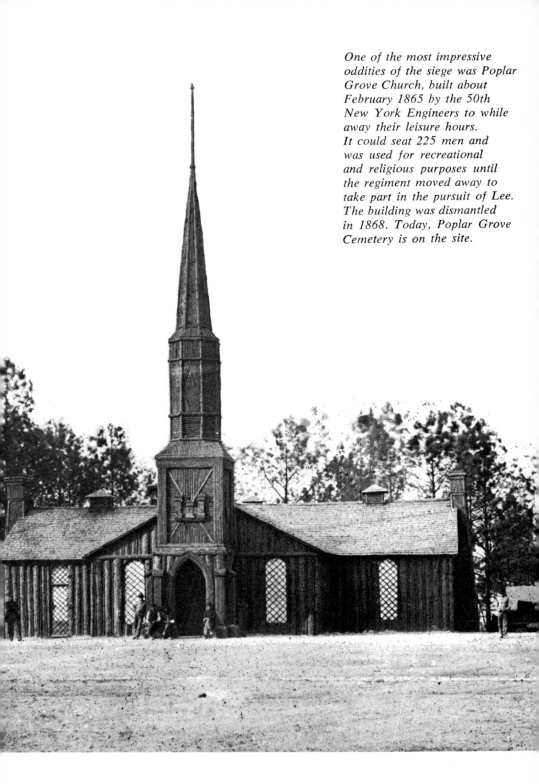

One of the most impressive
oddities of the siege was Poplar
Grove Church, built about
February 1865 by the 50th
New York Engineers to while
away their leisure hours.
It could seat 225 men and
was used for recreational
and religious purposes until
the regiment moved away to
take part in the pursuit of Lee.
The building was dismantled
in 1868. Today, Poplar Grove
Cemetery is on the site.

burg, which continued day by day with the addition of a few more feet or yards of picket line and rifle-pits, there had occurred five important thrusts aimed by the Northern leaders at encircling the city. They included two attacks on the Weldon Railroad, in June and August 1864; Peebles' Farm, in September and October; Boydton Plank Road, in October; and, finally, the move to Hatcher's Run in February 1865. They met with varying degrees of success, but still the Union noose was not drawn tightly enough.

The enlisted men of both armies, however, remained largely unaware of the strategy of their commanders. Their daily existence during the campaign took on a marked flavor, different in many respects from the more dashing engagements which preceded it. Too often war is a combination of bloodshed and boredom, and Petersburg, unlike most other military operations of the Civil War, had more than its share of the latter. The Petersburg episode—assault and resistance—dragged on to become the longest unbroken campaign against a single American city in the history of the United States. The romantic and heroic exploits were relatively few, and between them came long stretches of uninspiring and backbreaking routine.

The men of both sides had much in common, despite the bitterness with which they fought. In battle they were enemies, but in camp they were on the same common level. Stripped of the emotional tension and exhilaration of combat they all appear as bored, war-weary, homesick men. The greater part of their time was primarily utilized by digging and constructing fortifications, performing sentry and picket duty, and striving to speed up the long succession of days. They lived in rude improvised shelters, often made of mud and log walls with tent roofs. Chimneys were made of mud and barrels. There was some friendly interchange of words and gifts between the lines, but enmity was more rampant than brotherly regard. Off duty, the amusements and pastimes of the soldiers were simple and few—limited in most cases to their ability to improvise them. The most striking difference between the armies as the Petersburg campaign lengthened was that, while the

In late 1864, with food and supplies dwindling, desertion in the Confederate ranks became a major problem. This Southern cavalryman, completely discouraged and in rags, was one of those who crossed the lines to surrender. By early 1865, more than 2,000 Confederates had followed his example. One Union officer concluded that "if we stay here, the Johnnies will all come over before the 4th of July."

During the Civil War, a handful of "special artists" followed the Federal armies to supply glimpses of soldier life to news- and picture-hungry readers of such popular publications as the New York Illustrated News, Harper's Weekly, and Frank Leslie's Illustrated Newspaper. *Artists Edwin Forbes and the Waud brothers, Alfred and William, caught these scenes during the siege of Petersburg.*

1. Pickets trading between the lines. At quiet moments, opposing pickets sometimes met between the lines to trade coffee, tobacco, newspapers, and trinkets.

2. The wagon camp at night. Necessary but thankless was the task of the teamsters, those thousands of soldiers and civilians who drove the supply wagons from the railroads and ships to the front line. Theirs may have been a relatively safe job, but a bone-wearying one.

3. Pennsylvania soldiers voting, 1864. Volunteers considered themselves citizens first, soldiers second. These men, and thousands like them, took time out from their deadly work to vote in the Presidential election, doubtless, as the campaign song ran, "For Lincoln and Liberty, too."

4. Bivouac in the rifle-pits. Life in the infantry line was anything but pleasant: steaming, stinking mud in summer, frozen muck in winter. These soldiers of the V Corps built wood-and-canvas "shebangs" over their trenches as protection against the elements.

Northerners suffered most from boredom, the Confederates were plagued by the demoralizing effects of hunger.

The Petersburg campaign was grim business. Amusements could lighten the heart for only a brief time at best. Ever present were the mud and disease which followed every Civil War camp. Both opposing forces felt the chill of winter and the penetrating rain. The discour-

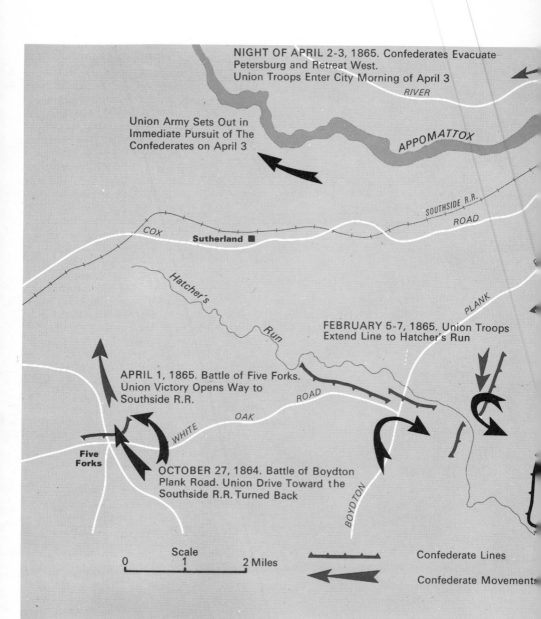

NIGHT OF APRIL 2-3, 1865. Confederates Evacuate Petersburg and Retreat West. Union Troops Enter City Morning of April 3

RIVER

Union Army Sets Out in Immediate Pursuit of The Confederates on April 3

APPOMATTOX

SOUTHSIDE R.R.

ROAD

COX

Sutherland ■

Hatcher's Run

PLANK

FEBRUARY 5-7, 1865. Union Troops Extend Line to Hatcher's Run

APRIL 1, 1865. Battle of Five Forks. Union Victory Opens Way to Southside R.R.

ROAD

OAK

WHITE

Five Forks

OCTOBER 27, 1864. Battle of Boydton Plank Road. Union Drive Toward the Southside R.R. Turned Back

BOYDTON

Scale
0   1   2 Miles

Confederate Lines

Confederate Movements

agement of the homesick, who never knew when, or if, they would return to their homes, was a hardship not peculiar to any rank. However, when spring came to warm the air, there was a difference between the two opposing armies. It was more than a numerical superiority. Then the Union soldiers felt confidence, while the Southern veterans, ill-clothed, ill-fed, and nearly surrounded, knew only despair.

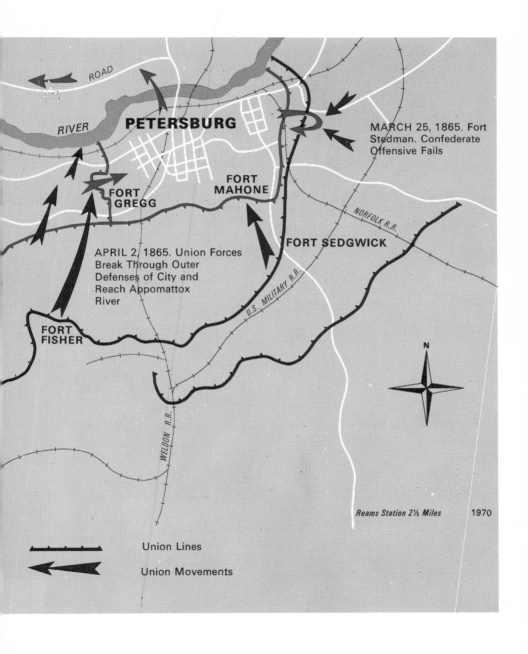

From June 1864 until April 1865, City Point was the "busiest place in Dixie." While Lee's outnumbered Confederates fought and starved behind their slowly crumbling defenses at Petersburg, here, just 8 miles away, Grant built up one of the largest supply depots of the Civil War which, during the 10 months of its existence, kept his army the best-fed, best-clothed, and best-munitioned in the field.

4

Explosion at City Point

5

1–4. Scenes at City Point,
Va., showing some of the
supplies and munitions
destined for Grant's army.
An Episcopal bishop from
Atlanta, visiting Grant at
City Point, was awed by the
abundance of military stores
that he saw—"not merely
profusion, but extravagance;
wagons, tents, artillery, ad
libitum. Soldiers provided
with everything."
5. On August 9, 1864, a
Confederate spy slipped
a time bomb on board one of
the ammunition barges
tied up at City Point. The
bomb's explosion, sketched
by A. R. Waud, killed or
wounded 200 people and
demolished more than 600
feet of warehouses and about
180 feet of wharf. Grant
himself was shaken up by
the blast, and one of his staff
members was wounded.

LEE'S LAST GAMBLE

By mid-March 1865 the climax of the campaign, and of the war, was close at hand. Lee's forces in both Richmond and Petersburg had dwindled to about 55,000. Grant, on the other hand, had available, or within easy march, at least 150,000. Moreover, Sheridan, having destroyed the remnants of Early's forces at Waynesboro, Va., on March 2, had cleared the Shenandoah Valley of Confederates and was now free to rejoin Grant before Petersburg.

Everywhere Lee turned, the military situation was black. Union forces under Sherman, driving the Confederates before them, had turned north from Savannah and were now hammering Johnston's forces in North Carolina. With President Jefferson Davis' consent, Lee sent a letter to General Grant on March 2 suggesting an interview. In the early morning hours of the second day following the dispatch of the letter, Lee and Maj. Gen. John B. Gordon discussed the three possible solutions to the problem which perplexed them: (1) Try to negotiate satisfactory peace terms. (This had already been acted upon in Lee's note to Grant.) (2) Retreat from Richmond and Petersburg and unite with Johnston for a final stand. (3) Attack Grant in order to facilitate retreat.

There followed a series of interviews with Confederate government officials in Richmond. Each of the plans was analyzed. The first was quickly dropped when Grant made it clear that he was not empowered to negotiate. Nor was the second proposal, that of retreat, deemed advisable by President Davis who wished to strike one more blow before surrendering his capital. This left only the third alternative—to attack.

Before settling on a definite course of action, however, Lee ordered General Gordon to make a reconnaissance of the Federal lines around Petersburg to see if they could be broken anywhere. Gordon soon reported that the best place for an attack was at Fort Stedman, a Union work located near the City Point and Petersburg Railroad and only 150 yards to the east of a strongly fortified Confederate position named Colquitt's Salient. Lee agreed with Gordon's assessment and, on the night of March 23, told Gordon to make preparations for an attack on the fort.

In Petersburg, sometime in the autumn of 1864, Lee was photographed on his horse Traveller for the first time. Although determined to fight on until all hope was gone, already Lee knew the war was going badly and that his tired, hungry, dirty, and cold soldiers could not hold out for long against Grant's growing might.

About one-half of the besieged army would be used to charge the Union line in the vicinity of Fort Stedman. It was hoped that this would cause Grant to shorten his front by withdrawing his left flank to protect his endangered right. Then Lee could detach a portion of the Confederate army to send to the aid of Johnston as, with shorter lines, he would not need as many men in Petersburg. Should the attack fail, he would attempt to retreat with all his forces for a final stand with Johnston. This would be the last desperate gamble of the Army of Northern Virginia.

The details for the attack were worked out by Gordon. During the night preceding the assault, the obstructions before the Confederate lines were to be removed and the Union pickets overcome as quietly as possible. A group of 50 men were to remove the chevaux-de-frise and abatis protecting Fort Stedman; then three companies of 100 men each were to charge and capture the fort. When Stedman was safely in Confederate hands, these men were to pretend they were Union troops and, forming into three columns, were to rush to the rear to capture other positions.

The next step was to send a division of infantry to gain possession of the siege lines north and south of the fallen bastion. When the breach had been sufficiently widened, Southern cavalry were to rush through and destroy telegraphic communication with Grant's headquarters at City Point. They were also ordered to cut the military railroad. Additional reserves were to follow the cavalry.

The attack was scheduled for the morning of March 25. The 50 axmen and the 300 soldiers who were to make up the advance columns were given strips of white cloth to wear across their chests to tell friend from foe. The officers in charge were given the names of Union officers known to be in the vicinity and were told to shout their assumed names if challenged. Beginning about 3 a.m., Confederates professing to be deserters crossed to the Union pickets offering to surrender. Their purpose: to be near at hand to overwhelm the unsuspecting pickets when the attack began.

At 4 a.m. Gordon gave the signal, and the Confederates sprang forward. At first the attack went as planned. Blue-clad pickets were silenced so effectively that not a shot was fired. Union obstructions were quickly hewn down by the axmen, and the small vanguard of 300 swept through Battery No. X which stood immediately north of Fort Stedman. They then rushed into the fort; the occupants were completely surprised and many surrendered without a fight. Battery XI to the south of Fort Stedman was also soon in Confederate hands. Union resistance in this early stage was ineffective, although Battery XI was recaptured for a short time.

More Confederates pressed into the torn line. While three columns set out in the general direction of City Point and along the Prince George Court House Road behind Stedman, other infantry units moved north and south along the Federal emplacements. To the north, they captured the fortifications as far as Battery IX where they were stopped by the Union defenders; to the south, they progressed as far as the ramparts of Fort Haskell. A desperate struggle ensued, but here, too, the

Maj. Gen. John B. Gordon planned and led the March 25 attack on Fort Stedman, one of the most advanced works on the Union line.

Northerners refused to yield. Despite these checks, the Confederates were now in possession of almost 1 mile of the Union line.

In the center of the Confederate attack, the three small columns quickly advanced as far as Harrison's Creek— a small stream which winds its way north to the Appomattox River 650 yards behind Fort Stedman. One of the columns succeeded in crossing the stream and continuing toward a small Union artillery post on the site of what had been Confederate Battery 8 (renamed Fort Friend by the Federals), but canister from the post forced the column back to the creek. Confusion took hold of the Confederates who were unable to locate the positions they had been ordered to capture behind the Union line. Artillery fire from Northern guns on a ridge to the east held them on the banks of Harrison's Creek. By 6 a.m. their forward momentum had been checked.

Union infantry then charged from the ridge to attack the Southerners. The forces joined battle along Harrison's Creek and the Confederates were soon forced back to Fort Stedman. For a brief time they held their newly captured positions. At 7:30 a.m. Brig. Gen. John F. Hartranft advanced on them with a division of Northern

troops. Heavy small-arms and artillery fire on Gordon's men threatened them with annihilation unless they retired to their own lines. About 8 a.m., Gordon received an order from Lee to withdraw his men. The order was quickly dispatched across the open fields to the soldiers in the captured Union works. By now, however, the line of retreat was raked by a vicious crossfire and many Confederates preferred surrender to withdrawal. About the same time Gordon was starting back, Hartranft ordered his division of Pennsylvania troops to recapture Fort Stedman. Within a few moments the Union line was completely restored and the forlorn Southern hope of a successful disruption of Northern communications, followed by secret withdrawal from the city, was lost. Equally bad, if not worse, to the Confederates was the loss of more than 4,000 killed, wounded, and captured as compared to the Union casualties of less than 1,500.

Of the three Confederate plans of action before the Battle of Fort Stedman, now only the second—retreat —was possible. The situation demanded immediate action, for, even as Gordon had been preparing on March 24 to launch his attack, Grant had been engaged in planning more difficulties for the harassed defenders of Petersburg.

Advancing from Colquitt's Salient (far left), Gordon's men captured Fort Stedman (left) but were driven out by a murderous crossfire from Federal artillery. In the assault, some 4,000 Confederates were killed, wounded, or captured.

FIVE FORKS: BEGINNING OF THE END

The coming of better weather heralded the opportunity for the final blows against the city. Grant, who was now passing some of the most anxious moments of his life, planned that this effort should be concentrated on the extreme right of the long Confederate line which protected Richmond and Petersburg. This meant that hostilities would soon commence somewhere west of Hatcher's Run, perhaps in the neighborhood of Dinwiddie Court House or a road junction called Five Forks which lay 17 miles southwest of Petersburg. On March 24, Grant ordered the II and IX Corps and three divisions of the Army of the James to the extreme left of the Union lines facing Lee. This resulted in a strong concentration northeast of Hatcher's Run. Two days later Sheridan arrived at City Point, fresh from his victorious campaign in the Shenandoah Valley, and was ordered to join his troops to those concentrated on the left. Finally, it began to appear that the Army of Northern Virginia was to be encircled.

Meanwhile, Lee was waiting only until he collected supplies and rations to last his men for a week and until the roads were passable before leaving to join Johnston. He hoped to leave on or about April 10. The information he received about the rapid accumulation of Union forces opposite his lightly held right was very disturbing, for, if it was true, the Federals not only threatened to cut off his retreat to the west and south, but they also posed a serious danger to the Southside Railroad—the last remaining communication link between Petersburg and the South, which continued to deliver a trickle of supplies to the city.

On March 29 the Union troops moved out. Sheridan's cavalry crossed the Rowanty Creek and occupied Dinwiddie Court House, while the II and V Corps crossed Hatcher's Run. In moving into position on the left of the II Corps, Warren's V Corps soldiers encountered heavy resistance north of Gravelly Run. While Sheridan was marshaling his troops around Dinwiddie, Lee issued orders on March 29 which sent Maj. Gens. George E. Pickett and Fitzhugh Lee to the Confederate right near Five Forks, far beyond Petersburg.

Sheridan was prepared to move against the Confeder-

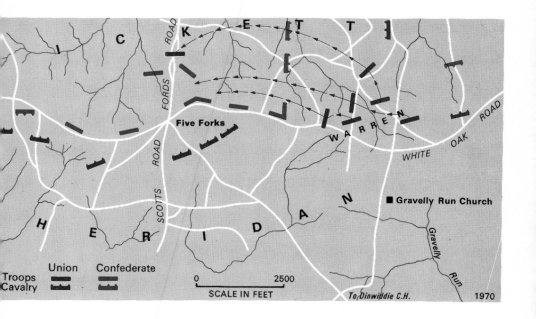

Troops
Cavalry
Union | Confederate

SCALE IN FEET
0   2500

To Dinwiddie C.H.

1970

ates with his cavalry on March 30, but heavy rains lasting from the evening of March 29 until the morning of the 31st made a large-scale movement impracticable over the muddy roads. On the last day of the month, part of Sheridan's forces which has pushed northwest toward Five Forks was attacked by Southern forces which succeeded in driving them back to Dinwiddie Court House, where Sheridan had a fresh division. Pickett then found his men badly outnumbered and withdrew them to Five Forks without pressing the advantage he had gained. This incident, called the Battle of Dinwiddie Court House, was a minor Confederate victory, although Sheridan's men were neither demoralized nor disorganized by the attack, and Robert E. Lee could find small comfort in the situation.

Meanwhile, there had been a savage clash on White Oak Road between Warren's V Corps and Maj. Gen. Bushrod Johnson's Confederate division. The Confederates at first swept all before them, but in the end numbers told and they were compelled to withdraw behind their breastworks.

The Confederates had been able to concentrate on their extreme right in the vicinity of Five Forks only about 10,000 cold and hungry soldiers to meet the expected Union drive to turn their right flank. Massed against this force commanded by Pickett were about 10,000 Northern cavalry and 12,000 infantry. The desperate urgency of General Lee's fears was indicated in the dispatch he sent to Pickett early on April 1, the day of the struggle for Five Forks: *"Hold Five Forks at all hazards*. Protect road to Ford's Depot and prevent Union forces from striking the south-side railroad. Regret exceedingly your forced withdrawal, and your inability to hold the advantage you had gained."

Throughout April 1, Pickett's troops worked unceasingly, erecting barricades of logs and earth around Five Forks. About 4 p.m., with only 2 hours of daylight remaining, Sheridan's cavalry and Warren's infantry attacked. While the cavalry occupied the attention of the Confederate defenders along White Oak Road, divisions of infantrymen from the V Corps moved to the left of Pickett's troops and, after crossing the White Oak Road which connected Five Forks with Petersburg, hit them on the weakly held left flank. Lacking sufficient artillery support, infantry reserves, and the presence of their commander, the Southerners were quickly overcome. Realizing that their position was no longer tenable, portions of the Confederate troops tried to retreat to Petersburg, but the avenue of escape had been cut by the Union advance across the White Oak Road.

By dusk, the Battle of Five Forks had ended. Union troops were in possession of the disputed area. They had cut off and captured more than 3,200 prisoners, while suffering a loss of probably less than 1,000.

Now the besieging forces were in position for the first time to accomplish Grant's objective of cutting Lee's supply lines and breaking through his fortifications. The western end of Lee's mobile defenses had crumbled.

Those Confederates who had survived the Battle of Five Forks had fallen back to the Southside Railroad where

When Maj. Gen. Philip H. Sheridan (above) sent cavalry and infantry crashing into the Confederate right flank at Five Forks on April 1, 1865, the Southern commander, Maj. Gen. George E. Pickett (left), was at a shad bake in the rear. By the time Pickett returned to his command, both it and the defense line had crumbled. Suddenly, Petersburg was no longer tenable. "It has happened as I told them in Richmond it would happen," said Lee. "The line has been stretched until it is broken."

67

they rallied for a stand, but darkness had prevented a Union pursuit. Grant's troops were within striking distance of the rail line, located less than 3 miles from Five Forks. Lee now knew that Petersburg and Richmond must be evacuated without delay or the Army of Northern Virginia would be completely cut off from outside help and all possible escape routes would be gone.

The problem of assigning a proper significance to Five Forks is a difficult one. It is now known that Lee and the Confederate government officials were on the verge of abandoning their capital. In June of the previous year the Southside Railroad had been a most important objective of the invading army, but the plight of Lee's army had grown so desperate during the intervening months that whether the railroad remained open or not mattered little. Grant, of course, did not know this as a positive fact, although the uncomfortable situation of his opponents was something of which he was doubtless aware. The real importance of Five Forks lay in the probability that, by making it more difficult for Lee to escape, it brought the inevitable a little closer. Lt. Col. Horace Porter, of Grant's staff, was positive more than 30 years later that news of Sheridan's success prompted the Union commander in chief to issue the orders for the attack that carried the city.

FALL OF PETERSBURG AND RICHMOND

Continuously throughout the night following the Battle of Five Forks, the Union artillery played upon the Confederate earthworks and dropped shells into the city. Troops were prepared for a general assault ordered for the following dawn. At 4:40 a.m., April 2, 1865, a frontal attack began with the sound of a signal gun from Fort Fisher. A heavy ground fog added to the confusion as the Federals drove in the Confederate pickets, cut away the abatis, and stormed over the works.

The story of the fighting along the Petersburg front on that spring Sunday is one of Union success over stout Confederate resistance. Maj. Gen. Horatio G. Wright's Union VI Corps broke through the works defended by troops of A. P. Hill's Corps and rolled up the Confederate line to right and left, while several regiments rushed on toward the Southside Railroad. Other elements of Grant's army swept away the remnants of the Confederate lines along Hatcher's Run. General Hill was killed early in the day by a Union soldier near the Boydton Plank Road while on the way to rally his men at Hatcher's Run.

The desperateness of the Southern position was shown when, about 10 a.m., Lee telegraphed President Davis to inform him of the turn of events at Petersburg. The message read: "I advise that all preparations be made for leaving Richmond tonight." Davis received the message while attending Sunday services at St. Paul's Church. He left immediately, destroying the calm of worship, to prepare for evacuating the capital. The flight of the Confederate government was promptly begun.

By midday the entire outer line to the west of Petersburg had been captured, with the exception of Fort Gregg. The city was now completely surrounded except to the north. The left of the Union line finally rested on the bank of the Appomattox River after months of strenuous effort.

It now became apparent to Lee that he must hold an inner line west of Petersburg until nightfall, when it would be possible for him to retreat from the city. While gray-clad troops were forming along this line built on the banks of Old Indian Town Creek, the defenders of Fort Gregg put up a stubborn delaying action against the Northern advance. Approximately 300 men and two pieces of artillery met an onslaught of 5,000 Northerners. The outcome of the struggle was determined by the numbers in the attacking force, but the capture of Fort Gregg occurred only after bitter hand-to-hand combat. The purpose of the defense had been accomplished, however, for a thin but sturdy line running behind them from Battery 45 to the Appomattox River had been manned. Temporarily, at least, street fighting within Petersburg had been avoided.

Blows directed at other points, such as Fort Mahone on the Jerusalem Plank Road, were slowed after troops of Maj. Gen. John G. Parke's IX Corps had captured 12 guns and 400 yards of the Confederate line to the right and left of the road. Desperate counterattacks by

Gordon's Confederates kept the Federals from exploiting this breakthrough. Yet there was no doubt in the minds of Lee and other Southern leaders that all hope of retaining Petersburg and Richmond was gone. It was obvious that, if the lines held the Union army in check on April 2, they must be surrendered on the morrow. The object was to delay until evening, when retreat would be possible.

The close of the day found the weary Confederates concentrating within Petersburg and making all possible plans to withdraw. Lee had issued the necessary instructions at 5 o'clock that afternoon. By 8 p.m. the retreat was under way, the artillery preceding the infantry across the Appomattox River. Amelia Court House, 40 miles to the west, was designated as the assembly point for the troops from Petersburg and Richmond.

Grant had ordered the assault on Petersburg to be renewed early on April 3. It was discovered at 3 a.m. that the Southern earthworks had been abandoned; an attack was not necessary. Union troops took possession of the city shortly after 4 o'clock in the morning. Richmond officially surrendered 4 hours later.

President Lincoln, who had been in the vicinity of Petersburg for more than a week, came from army headquarters at City Point that same day for a brief visit with Grant. They talked quietly on the porch of a private house for 1½ hours before the President returned to City Point. Grant, with all of his army, except the detachments necessary to police Petersburg and Richmond and to protect City Point, set out in pursuit of Lee. He left Maj. Gen. George L. Hartsuff in command at Petersburg.

Petersburg had fallen, but it was at a heavy price. In the absence of complete records, the exact casualties will never be known, but in the 10-month campaign at least 42,000 Union soldiers had been killed, wounded, and captured, while the Confederates had suffered losses of more than 28,000. Although the northern forces had lost more men than their opponents, they had been able to replenish them more readily. Moreover, Grant had been prepared to utilize the greater resources at his disposal, and the Petersburg campaign had been turned

1

2

1. *Fort Mahone after its capture, 1865.*

2. *Deserted Confederate huts on the abandoned Petersburg line.*

by him into a form of relentless attrition which the Southern army had not been able to stand. The result had been the capture of Petersburg and Richmond, but more important, it had led to the flight of the remnants of the once mighty Army of Northern Virginia.

On the Sunday following the evacuation of Petersburg and Richmond, Lee's troops were cut off at Appomattox Court House, destroying any hopes they might have had for uniting with Johnston in North Carolina. In this small Virginia town nearly 100 miles west of Petersburg, the Army of Northern Virginia, now numbering little more than 28,000, surrendered to the Union forces. Within a week of the fall of Petersburg the major striking force of the Confederacy had capitulated. General Johnston surrendered his army to General Sherman in North Carolina on April 26. By early June 1865, all Confederate forces had been surrendered, and the Civil War was over.

Union soldiers on Sycamore Street in Petersburg, April 1865. For these men, basking in the aftermath of a successful campaign, the war is almost over. To the west, General Sheridan's cavalry is racing to cut off the retreating Southern army. "If the thing is pressed," Sheridan tells Grant, "I think Lee will surrender." Says Lincoln: "Let the thing be pressed."

On April 3, 1865, with
Petersburg in Union hands
at last, General Grant issued
orders sending off the
Armies of the Potomac and
the James in pursuit of Lee.
While the photographer was
taking this picture, showing a
Federal wagon train leaving
the city to join in the chase,
the remnants of Lee's army
were marching toward a
little crossroad village named
Appomattox Court House.

FOR FURTHER READING: Bruce Catton, *Grant Takes Command,* Boston, 1969 / Bruce Catton, *A Stillness at Appomattox,* New York, 1953 / Douglas Southall Freeman, *Lee's Lieutenants: A Study in Command,* 3 vols., New York, 1942-46, vol. III / Douglas Southall Freeman, *R. E. Lee, A Biography,* 4 vols., New York, 1934-35, vols. III and IV / Ulysses S. Grant, *Personal Memoirs,* 2 vols., New York, 1885-86, vol. II / Andrew A. Humphreys, *The Virginia Campaign of 1864 and 1865,* New York, 1883 / Robert U. Johnson and Clarence C. Buel, eds., *Battles and Leaders of the Civil War,* 4 vols., New York, 1887 (reissued, 1956), vol. IV / Theodore Lyman, *Meade's Headquarters, 1863-1865: Letters of Colonel Theodore Lyman from the Wilderness to Appomattox,* edited by George R. Agassiz, Boston, 1922 / Francis Trevelyan Miller, ed., *The Photographic History of the Civil War,* 10 vols., New York, 1911 (reissued, 1957) / Henry Pleasants, Jr., *The Tragedy of the Crater,* Boston, 1936 / Horace Porter, *Campaigning With Grant,* New York, 1897 (reissued, 1961) / Benjamin Quarles, *The Negro in the Civil War,* Boston, 1953 / Philip Van Doren Stern, *An End to Valor: The Last Days of the Civil War, Boston,* 1958 / William Swinton, *Campaigns of the Army of the Potomac,* New York, 1882 / U.S. War Department, *War of the Rebellion: A Compilation of the Official Records of the Union and Confederate Armies,* 128 vols., Washington, 1880-1901, Series I, vols. 36, 38, 40, 46, 51; Series III, vol. 5.

NATIONAL PARK SERVICE HISTORY SERIES: Antietam / Aztec Ruins / Bandelier / Campaign for Petersburg / Chalmette / Chickamauga and Chattanooga Battlefields / Custer Battlefield / Custis-Lee Mansion, the Robert E. Lee Memorial / Ford's Theatre and the House Where Lincoln Died / Fort Davis / Fort Laramie / Fort McHenry / Fort Necessity / Fort Pulaski / Fort Raleigh / Fort Sumter / Fort Union / Fredericksburg Battlefields / George Washington Birthplace / Gettysburg / Golden Spike / Guilford Courthouse / Hopewell Village / Independence / Jamestown, Virginia / Kings Mountain / Manassas (Bull Run) / Montezuma Castle / Morristown, A Military Capital of the Revolution / Ocmulgee / Richmond Battlefields / Saratoga / Scotts Bluff / Shiloh / Statue of Liberty / Vanderbilt Mansion / Vicksburg / Whitman Mission / Wright Brothers / Yorktown

Pricelists of Park Service publications sold by the Government Printing Office may be obtained from the Superintendent of Documents, Washington, DC 20402.

ADMINISTRATION: Petersburg National Battlefield is administered by the National Park Service, U.S. Department of the Interior. A superintendent, whose address is Box 549, Petersburg, VA 23803, is in immediate charge / As the Nation's principal conservation agency, the Department of the Interior has basic responsibilities for water, fish, wildlife, mineral, land, park, and recreational resources. Indian and Territorial affairs are other major concerns of America's "Department of Natural Resources." The Department works to assure the wisest choice in managing all our resources so each will make its full contribution to a better United States—now and in the future.

U.S. DEPARTMENT OF THE INTERIOR   NATIONAL PARK SERVICE

☆ U.S. GOVERNMENT PRINTING OFFICE : 1975 O—595-548